How to Overcome Obstacles

Effective strategies on how to overcome obstacles to unlock full potential

Francis Don

Table of Contents

Introduction

Scrolling through social media, you surely see a dozen picture-perfect lifestyles that don't reflect your own. When browsing, you probably feel your life doesn't live up to others, particularly when a struggle or pain comes your way.

I'm going to let you in on a little secret, however. Everyone confronts difficulties. Whether or not they want to reveal those difficulties for other people to see is up to them. Instead of lingering on comparing your challenges to others, it's more effective to concentrate on yourself, gear your mentality to conquer the obstacle, and transform it into success.

But how can one achieve that? Many difficulties seem intimidating and hard to surmount. As a result, it is simple to grow disillusioned or give up on the problem completely. Or, like some individuals, you may feel resentful of those who appear to conquer any obstacle and transform it into success with ease.

Giving up and bitterness are pointless. By altering your perspective, you may become someone who converts challenges into success. Don't get me wrong, it will take a lot of hard work, perseverance, blood, sweat, and tears, but you too can conquer any difficulties and change them into success.

In this book, we're going to explain to you how to accomplish it. We begin by looking at what obstacles are and how you should view them.

From there, we look at critical aspects like why perception matters and the extent of influence you have over obstacles. These first few chapters are critical for creating a firm basis for conquering problems.

Next, we provide you with the two most critical actions for actively conquering your obstacles, including recognizing them and creating objectives for direct action. Finally, we close by emphasizing the significance of concentrating on yourself, emotional resilience, and continuing practice.

Together, these chapters provide you with a critical blueprint for not only conquering one difficulty in your life but how to learn from your challenges so that you may transform each struggle you meet into success.

Whether you are experiencing a major obstacle at present time or wish to change your life, use this book as a roadmap for changing any struggle into a success. Let's get started.

Chapter 1

THE TRUTH ABOUT OBSTACLES

Before diving into how to overcome obstacles, you need to know about the reality of them.

Everyone understands what an obstacle is, but most have an unrealistic and skewed view of it. Instead of seeing difficulties as chances for progress, individuals regard them as events acting against them. This erroneous concept makes it much more difficult to conquer your obstacle and change it into success.

With that in mind, you need to realize the truth about obstacles; obstacles are not all terrible. I realize this thought may seem a bit extreme, but it is true.

Just like everything else in life, difficulties come with both pros and cons. Recognizing all sides can help you solve the problem swiftly and effectively.

Why Looking at Both the Negatives and Positives Matters

Whenever an obstacle comes your way, it is crucial to remember this reality. If you concentrate on the negatives, as most people do, it is much simpler to feel distressed, overwhelmed, and disheartened by the circumstance. This will make it tougher to conquer and transform it into success.

However, if you look at the negatives and the positives, you view the obstacle from a much more realistic perspective. This realistic grasp of problems helps you think reasonably and clearly about the work at hand. From there, you may begin to conquer your issue instead of feeling overwhelmed by it.

Not to mention, you take away most of the negatives of obstacles anytime you consider the pros. This will make it simpler and more pleasurable to combat your challenges, even if you aren't necessarily succeeding as soon as you want.

Possible Negatives of Obstacles

Obviously, obstacles come with various negatives. Even though you shouldn't be trapped in the negativity, you should be aware of them so that you know how to best go about your circumstance and conquer the obstacle. Whenever you are aware of the negatives, more of the power is given back to you.

As a result, you may begin to manage the obstacle since the negatives are your own. Acknowledging them merely makes them less terrifying.

The specific negatives of the obstacle will vary on the task. For example, your obstacle may be obtaining employment. In this case, the negatives can be that you are under financial hardship, need to relocate, or anything linked to the new job. These negatives are distinct from the negatives of a different difficulty, such relationship issues.

In addition to the obstacle focused negatives, certain negatives are prevalent in all obstacles. Most significantly, obstacles demand you to work. If you already have a full-time job and other duties, the extra duty of conquering the obstacle might take a lot of your time and energy, even for the most industrious individuals.

Not only that, but obstacles push you physically, psychologically, and emotionally. Every time you find yourself in a new obstacle, you are compelled to push yourself to improve as a person. This procedure takes up, once again, a lot of energy, and it might bring up a lot of unpleasant feelings depending on the scenario.

The physical effort and mental distress that comes with most obstacles are what make obstacles so dreadful. Most individuals don't appreciate more effort. So, they grow to hate obstacles.

Guaranteed Positives of Obstacles

In addition to the negatives, obstacles have a lot of positives. Most individuals fail to perceive these positives, and they concentrate on the negatives. Though this is tremendously tempting to do, you should try your utmost to maintain the positives in your thoughts. The positives will help you overcome the challenges, remain motivated, and enjoy the process.

Forces You to Grow

The greatest benefit of every obstacle is that it forces you to improve. Even if challenges come with a lot of hard work and effort, it is the only way for you to become the person you want to be. In other words, trials make you a better person.

Some obstacles may make you physically better, such as an unforeseen health crisis, while others may make you emotionally more robust. It doesn't matter how the challenge helps you develop. What's important is that you improve and become a better person at the end of it all.

Helps You to Get to Know Yourself Better

Another benefit to coming out of obstacles is that you come to know yourself better. We are typically instructed to get to know our colleagues, family members, and friends, but we often forget to know ourselves. This makes it more difficult for us to trust our thinking and know what we want out of life. Obstacles compel us to reflect on ourselves and the world. It teaches us our strengths, shortcomings, and limitations. This permits us to come to know ourselves in a manner that would not be possible without obstacles.

Improves Self-Esteem

As we mature and come to know ourselves better, our self-esteem increases as well. So, obstacles lead to enhanced self-esteem, which is their third benefit. Self-esteem allows us to realize our worth outside of our achievements and abilities. It is vital for a happy and functional existence.

Improves Relationships

The last benefit of obstacles is that they may strengthen our relationships. You presumably have observed that persons with similar struggles tend to be some of your strongest and most trusted connections. As you go through problems, you become more empathic and able to relate with other individuals in similar circumstances.

Recap

All in all, obstacles are not entirely negative things. Even though they are a lot of effort and may put pressure on your life, they drive you to develop, assist you to get to know yourself, enhance your self-esteem, and strengthen your relationships. Remembering these positives and the negatives will help you conquer the challenge because of your practical and sensible thinking.

Chapter 2

PERCEPTION MATTERS

One thing that we talked on in the previous chapter but didn't clearly explore is the problem of perception. Our perceptions are how we perceive events or persons based on our sensory experiences. Even if our perceptions are all we know, how we see an event may not be true to how it unfolds in reality.

Probably enough, we can never escape our impressions, no matter how hard we try. Perceptions impact every single facet of our day-to-day lives. How we view the environment ultimately influences many of our situations and feelings.

Because of how essential perception is in our lives, your view of the problem will primarily decide how you manage it and whether or not you can overcome it.

Enhance your perception of obstacles to help you transform any obstacle into success.

What Psychology Says About Perception

Psychology has done a lot of research on perception. As we just discussed, psychology determines that our perception is affected by our sensory experience with the world, meaning our sense of sight, smell, touch, and more.

More so, psychology has revealed that it impacts how we react to our problems. For example, if we negatively regard obstacles, we are more inclined to quit and feel discouraged by them. In contrast, having an optimistic mentality regarding obstacles makes us more likely to overcome the obstacle and succeed.

The most valuable thing psychology informs us about perception is that we have some control. Though it is hard to have perfect control, we may somewhat shift our views by paying attention, consciously translating our perception into meaning, behaving appropriately, and practicing with our new mindset.

- Pay attention: What is your perception of an event? How does it differ from reality? How do you know?
- Give your perception meaning: What does it mean to you? Do you agree with this meaning? Should you change the meaning?
- Act accordingly: How do my actions reflect my view of the situation?
- Practice: What are ways that I can incorporate this new mindset into my everyday life?

What this implies for obstacles is that you may change your negative view or mentality into a positive one. Simply with focused and devoted activity, you might find yourself more likely to achieve by altering your thinking.

As you are actively working to change your thinking, it is helpful to assess your progress by keeping notes or utilizing some software. Continue to behave in line with this new thinking and measure your development. Stay positive even when it's hard, and you will begin to notice your perspective transform.

Popular Mindsets

Since perception matters, you are probably wondering what type of mindset you should have. There are three prevalent mindsets, but only one will lead to long-term success. The fixed mindset, mixed mindset, and growth mindset are all three prevalent mindsets that individuals unwittingly hold.

Fixed Mindset

The fixed mindset informs us that we are born with abilities and skills. We cannot actually improve upon our skills, meaning our success is totally up to our DNA. For example, a fixed mindset might convince you that you can never achieve a decent mark in school as you are not clever.

This thinking is immensely common, yet it is destructive. It takes away any influence over our own situations and blames it on our natural talents. Not only that, but the fixed mindset is false.

In the scenario stated in the previous paragraph, a student feels they can never obtain a decent score because they are not clever. Except for serious learning problems, most kids can receive a decent grade with hard work and effort, even if they aren't the most naturally clever. This reveals the fixed mindset to be false.

Growth Mindset

The reverse of the fixed mindset is the growth mindset. The growth mentality reminds you that you have some innate talents and capabilities, but you can foster your deficiencies and improve as a person. For example, a growth mindset may inform you that you aren't the greatest at arithmetic, but you can progress with devotion and hard effort.

The growth mentality is by far the greatest attitude for overcoming problems and being successful. It keeps you from being overwhelmed and quitting when presented with a new issue. Instead, it enables you to remain focused and driven to develop yourself.

If you want to conquer any problem, you need to start adjusting your thinking from a fixed one to a growth version.

Mixed Mindset

In the process of transitioning from a fixed mindset to a growth mindset, you will likely find yourself with a mixed attitude. A mixed mindset is one that is in between a fixed and growth one. Sometimes, you may find yourself thinking in fixed terms, but you will find yourself thinking in growth terms at other times.

Even if you aren't where you want to be when you find yourself with a mixed mindset, it is an improvement from before. You should be delighted that you are making progress; keep up the hard work. Continue to monitor your development and consciously maintain a growth mindset to break away from your fixed way of thinking totally.

Recap

When it comes to challenges, perception may make or break you. Though it is simple to have a fixed mindset, a growth mindset can help you overcome any challenge and convert it into success. Track your progress, operate with a growth mindset in your vision, and remain hopeful to change your fixed thinking into possibilities for growth.

Chapter 3

YOU'RE NOT IN CONTROL

In addition to mindset and perception, the way you view control will primarily decide whether you conquer your problem. The delusion that we are in charge is primarily responsible for many of the obstacles we find ourselves confronting, although the obstacle is illusionary.

First and foremost, we have to accept that we are not as in control as we would want. As humans, we naturally want control over our whole lives. Despite this overwhelming drive to be in control, we are only in charge of very little.

By attempting to manage things that are utterly beyond our range of control, many obstacles appear overpowering and scary. That's because they are. Viewing oneself as in control produces many made-up obstacles that we have no means of overcoming. It is crucial to learn this lesson if you want to overcome challenges.

Knowing When To Let Go

Because of this control problem, many of us cling to obstacles that we have no business holding on to. These will be obstacles that we have no hope of overcoming.

Whenever we strive to conquer obstacles we can't fight, we feel overwhelmed and blame ourselves. Most likely, your incapacity to overcome an obstacle has nothing to do with you but the circumstances of the case.

With this in mind, it is crucial to remember that you should not get caught up in things that are not in your control. Focusing on things beyond your control wastes your time and energy and may affect your self-esteem. Only concentrate on things that you have at least some control over.

Whenever you find yourself facing an obstacle that you aren't sure whether you should control, you may want to evaluate it. If you cannot influence the obstacle result in any way, let go of it. Knowing whether or not you should let go might be tough, but there are two factors to consider:

1. The facts
2. Your emotions

The facts of the obstacle and your emotions will decide whether or not you are in charge of the result and whether you should let go of it. The realities of the obstacle include anything that is a prerequisite for the obstacle to be overcome.

For example, assume your obstacle is that you have been sacked and need money. The facts would include how long you can survive without an income, the number of individuals dependent on you, and anything else that can be objectively verified.

In addition to the facts, you need to examine your feelings. Your emotions will mostly decide whether the challenge is worth it to you. Sometimes, the obstacle is under your hands, and the facts enable you to overcome it. Nevertheless, your emotions may tell you that the difficulty is not worth it.

Let's look at an example. Assume that your spouse obtains a new job and must relocate across the nation. The difficulty in front of you is whether or not you should relocate or be in a long-distance relationship.

Both of these possibilities are achievable, but your emotions may tell you that you don't want to relocate and you can't accept a long-distance relationship. In such a situation, your emotions tell you that this difficulty is not worth overcoming and that you should perhaps split up.

By looking at the facts and your feelings, you should be able to assess whether a challenge is worth it. If the obstacle is not, give it up and go on with your life. Though this may require a lot of courage and endurance, it will make your life much simpler.

How to Let Go of Control

To carry on, you have to realize and let go of control. For most individuals, this might not be easy. Here are some helpful actions to help you let go of control and go back to living a life you like.

Focus on What You Can Control

The first step to letting go of control is to concentrate on what you can control and acknowledge what you can't. What you can control solely pertains to you, and the list is quite small. Your appearance, mindfulness, aspects of your health, and productivity are examples of things that are under your control. Any circumstance that includes another person is not fully under your control. You can control how you react to the other person, but you cannot control how they behave or react.

Notice Your Reaction Pattern

Your reaction pattern is how you respond to another person or scenario. Most of the time, our emotions lead to our responses. This isn't inherently negative, but it might imply that you respond poorly, which undermines your capacity to conquer the obstacle.

Notice your reaction pattern to influence the outcome. Your reaction pattern will contain the trigger, stress reaction, negative thinking, negative mood, reactive activity, and the consequence. Take a second to ponder on this reaction pattern so that you know how you react.

If you believe that your reaction is weak and leads to undesirable consequences, you need to stop the pattern. This entails detecting the trigger, breathing, and being compassionate to yourself and others throughout the process. Additionally, change your negative thoughts into more realistic ones.

Changing your response pattern will offer you far more control over yourself. Still, it won't fully alter the event, but it will affect how you respond to it and your emotions.

Mantras

You may also use mantras to help let go of the control freak within you. Mantras are fast and beneficial sayings you chant to yourself throughout the day. Studies have proven that mantras work if you repeat them to yourself regularly.

They affect the way you think, and consequently, they influence the way you react. Here is a selection of useful mantras for letting go of control:

- I let go of the urge to dominate people.
- I let go of everything beyond my control.
- I control myself and my happiness.
- I only control myself and my emotions.

Recap

Our demand for control transforms things; we should let go of obstacles. Learn how to discern when obstacles are not worth your attention. Then, attempt to let go of your urge to control everything to go back to your life and only address problems that are worth your attention.

Chapter 4

IDENTIFYING OBSTACLES

Now that we have established the foundation for overcoming obstacles, we can delve into how to transform them into success. As with any other issue that may come your way, the first step to overcoming your obstacle is to recognize it. To put it another way, you need to know what the obstacle is and classify it.

Identifying the obstacle will make you more aware of the positives, negatives, your own biases, and what you need to do to overcome them. If you don't recognize your obstacle, it will be tough to come up with specific steps to follow. Though there are countless obstacles, many may be categorized into larger groups, such as confronting the unknown or limited finances.

In this chapter, we are going to take a look at the most popular categories for obstacles. You may observe that the obstacle in front of you is a blend of more than one group. That is perfectly natural. Let's take a look at what these frequent obstacle types are.

Facing the Unknown

One of the most general obstacle types is confronting the unknown. Facing the unknown occurs anytime you find yourself in a position that is uncharted terrain. Whenever you relocate, obtain a new job, or chat with a new person, you might find yourself confronting the unknown.

This obstacle will be particularly challenging for persons with nervousness, introverted dispositions, and poor self-esteem. That's because it takes a lot of courage and confidence to conquer this obstacle and make the unfamiliar familiar.

The simplest method to overcome this problem is to remind yourself that everyone has been in a similar circumstance before, and most people are not going to criticize you. Additionally, focus on your self-esteem to become more trusting in yourself and your capacity to act in the unknown.

Pressure to be Someone Other than Yourself

Another obstacle you may encounter is pressure to be someone other than yourself. This pressure might come from family, friends, or society. Some individuals struggle with this obstacle more than others. Women particularly confront this obstacle, but males do as well.

To overcome this obstacle, you need to know where to draw the boundary between yourself and others. What are your values? What do you think of yourself? What do you want out of life? Asking these types of questions will define where you end, and other people begin.

To overcome this challenge, you need to concentrate on boundary establishment. Once you draw the line and set a severe boundary between yourself and others, you have to have the confidence and commitment to follow through. You may need to focus on your self-confidence and self-esteem to preserve the boundaries.

Limited Finances

Limited finances are immensely challenging. In many circumstances, low resources are due to something beyond your control. Losing a career, bringing a new member of the family, an unforeseen injury, and more may all lead to a restricted financial impediment.

Unlike the last two obstacles, this one will demand far more real and clear action measures. This involves making a budget, calculating how much more money you need to earn, and more. It may also demand you to hunt for new employment or ask for a spouse to assist financially.

Along with the obvious challenges that come with limited finances, such as not paying a payment, there will also be reformation that you have to confront, such as strained relationships, facing the unknown, and more.

Relationship Problems

Relationships are one of the most frequent areas for challenges. As humans, we are all entitled to our opinions and deeds, yet we frequently assume that everyone should fall in line with our thoughts. As a consequence, a lot of tension may develop, and it is more difficult to overcome these obstacles as it includes other independent individuals. Often, an obstacle in a relationship is a very particular occurrence or trend. To identify the obstacle, you need to communicate with the other person to understand their side of the story. Work with the other person to identify action steps to remove the obstacle in the future.

Sometimes, the obstacle may be intractable. For example, your spouse may not desire children while you do. Often, the only option for overcoming this issue is separating and finding a new partner with the same ambition and desire for children as you.

You might also have obstacles due to conflicts with your friends, parents, or children, not only your romantic partner. Approach their resolution in the same approach.

What to Do After Identifying the Obstacle?

Once you identify the impediment, it is crucial to design action steps that are directly relevant to the situation at hand. Action steps offer you something practical to do to overcome the issue. Your action steps should not be too lofty, but they should instead be more like mini-goals. We shall discuss more of this in the subsequent chapters.

In addition to active steps, you may need to reflect on yourself. Certain challenges will take a big toll on your emotional and mental well-being. Reflect on yourself and pay attention to your feelings. Many individuals are inclined to set their emotions aside to conquer the obstacle swiftly.

Completely disregarding your emotions is just as harmful as being carried away by them. Consider your emotions and utilize them as guides for learning.

More frequently than you might imagine, the main obstacle is between your ears, not in the real world. Take the time to focus on yourself, your ambitions, and your aspirations to come to a strong knowledge of where you stand.

Recap

The first step to overcoming the obstacle is to identify the actual issue. You may achieve this by splitting the obstacle into categories, which will assist the obstacle to look more concrete in your mind. From there, build action steps and connect back to your emotions to seek a resolution actively.

Chapter 5

SET GOALS

As we discussed in the previous chapter, goals are an essential approach to overcoming obstacles and turning them into achievements. Goals are tougher than you would imagine, though. Many individuals are naive about goal setting and follow-through, making it tough to overcome obstacles.

In this chapter, we are going to look at how you should build up objectives to conquer your obstacles. These objectives might be termed SMART goals. Let's have a peek.

SMART Goals

The ideal sort of goal to establish is called SMART goals. SMART is an abbreviation for specific, measurable, attainable, realistic, and timely. Incorporating all five of these components into your objectives assures that they are manageable and that you are capable of accomplishing them.

A specific goal has one purpose in mind. It should be highly concentrated so that you have a definite idea of what you need to do. More than that, the exact aim has to be quantifiable. This implies that you need to be able to measure whether or not you accomplished the goal.

On top of that, it has to be both achievable and realistic. There is no point in setting a goal that you cannot achieve or that is entirely outside of your capabilities. Finally, select a time by which you need to fulfill the goal. This will keep you motivated.

For example, assume that the challenge in front of you is that you need to reduce weight. The objective should be to lose 25 pounds in 3 months. This weight reduction target of 25 pounds is specific, measurable, achievable, realistic, and timely.

What If I Can't Come up With a SMART Goal?

Say that you have been thinking about a SMART objective and keep coming up with nothing. If you find yourself in this circumstance, you might approach a close friend or family member for help. They may be able to offer you a fresh perspective that you hadn't thought about.

If you still aren't able to come up with a SMART goal, then the odds are that you do not have control of the issue. If you do not have control over it, then there is no way to make a goal to attain it. You may create objectives to reduce symptoms of the obstacle, but you can't guarantee success.

You can run into this dilemma if your obstacle concerns another individual. Say your spouse wants to leave you, and you don't want a divorce. Since there is another equally autonomous individual participating, you don't have entire control over the issue. As a consequence, you may not be able to develop SMART goals to assure success in the circumstance.

However, you may come up with SMART goals to assist you to get through the process or connect to your spouse better. Talk through the matter with your spouse to attempt to get on the same page. From there, develop targets to soften the blow. This may entail therapy, concentrating on your interests, or anything else that you have control over.

Follow Through

Your goals are worthless if you don't follow through with them. Once you establish your goals, find a means to inspire yourself to keep working at them. SMART goals are the greatest approach to keep up and remain motivated. Even with SMART goals, though, you have to keep working.

You could wish to create rewards for yourself after dividing up the SMART goal into smaller goals or mini-goals. Every time you accomplish a mini-goal, you reward yourself. This keeps you enthusiastic and eager to reach the next mini-goal.

Commit yourself. Many individuals create goals, but they don't fully commit to them. Ensure that you follow through by not allowing yourself the opportunity to slack. Just as you would hold someone else responsible for completing their commitments, hold yourself accountable as well.

Be Flexible

When talking about goals, we would be remiss not to discuss flexibility. When most people set goals, they are highly inflexible and unwilling to budge. This is nearly a certain method to fail and not conquer your problem. Instead, you need to be adaptable, even when it comes to ambitions.

Sometimes, plans change, obstacles change, or your priorities shift. When this occurs, you have to be able to alter your attention and goals to reflect this happening. If not, the objectives will be divorced from where you are in life. Too restrictive objectives are going to shatter eventually.

Instead of seeing goals as something inflexible, perceive them as fluid. Be strict in following through with your goals yet be open to adjusting them if you need to. Whenever the plans alter, flexible goals will bend with the strain instead of shattering.

Recap

Goals assist you to accomplish your obstacles. Set SMART goals to keep you motivated and more likely to transform your obstacles into achievement. Though you will need to commit to yourself and keep yourself accountable, objectives are truly the only way not to be wrecked by your obstacles.

Chapter 6

FOCUS ON YOURSELF

We cannot talk about overcoming obstacles without emphasizing the significance of concentrating on yourself and not comparing yourself to others. Because of social media and many other reasons nowadays, it is simpler than ever to compare oneself to someone else.

Doing this is damaging to our growth, success, and wellness. Not to mention, it makes conquering problems virtually impossible and places new obstacles in our way

To overcome obstacles, you have to quit this behavior quickly. Your overall health and welfare will change for the better. Though it is simple to compare yourself to others when confronting a challenge, you have to prevent it.

Why You Shouldn't Compare Yourself to Others?

The major reason you shouldn't compare yourself to others while conquering any challenge is to build additional obstacles in the process. In other words, it produces a mountain out of a molehill. If you are already anxious over the main obstacle, you don't want to make the procedure any tougher than it needs to be.

Additionally, comparing yourself to others may hamper your capacity to live the life you desire. When you compare yourself to someone else, you are experiencing yourself and them from their viewpoint. Doing so suggests that you aren't valuing your ideas and thoughts as seriously as you should.

If you continue to place someone else's values over your own, it may be hard to overcome an obstacle or build the life you desire. Only concentrate on yourself and quit comparing yourself to others to prevent this from occurring.

Comparing Yourself to Others Creates Unrealistic Notions

There are a few reasons why comparing oneself is not just harmful but unreasonable. Most importantly, you never get the complete picture while looking at someone from the outside. People desire to look better off than they are, so they only display the bright parts.

When you compare yourself to others, you are comparing yourself to an impossible standard. You aren't witnessing the trials, problems, or challenges they had to undergo to get to where they are. This leaves you with an erroneous idea of where you need to be.

Another reason why comparing yourself to others is unreasonable is that it just is not relevant to you. Even if you could get the complete picture, which you can't, it's not your life. To spend your energy comparing yourself to others is a sheer waste of time.

What Should You Do Instead?

Instead of comparing yourself to others, you should think about your ambitions and wants. This will give you a good notion of where you are and where you want to be. It is the most helpful and practical approach to overcoming any challenge.

If you have to compare yourself to someone, compare your present self to your prior self. You should have developed by now, and the fact you are taking so much effort to sever your comparison connections demonstrates that you have improved. Compare yourself against your prior self to enhance improvement.

Of course, it is OK to speak to other people and obtain their opinion. Other individuals have gone through similar experiences as you. Talk to them to discover what they say about the scenario. Don't follow their advice blindly, however. Compare it to your thoughts and goals and move from there.

Here are some techniques to quit comparing yourself to others:

Be Aware of Your Triggers

Be aware of your triggers, which are situations that make you feel inadequate, and encourage you to compare yourself to others. Triggers may be particular persons on social media or going into certain businesses. Be aware of your triggers so you know when you are prone to compare yourself to others.

Once you know where your triggers are, do your best to avoid them. It may be uncomfortable, but it is essential—to unfollow individuals that make you feel horrible about yourself or avoid areas that lead you to compare.

Remember You Don't See the Whole Story

Whenever you feel yourself falling up, realize that you don't see the whole situation. People will put up a front to make themselves look better than they feel. Remind yourself of this reality to assist in bringing you back to a more realistic perspective.

Be Grateful for Your Life

Finally, discover methods to demonstrate more gratitude for yourself in your own life. Look at everything you appreciate about your present life and repeat it to yourself. As you're compiling a list, you'll uncover much more things to adore than you first imagined.

If the excessive comparison is something you suffer from, you may want to start your morning or finish your day with this suggestion. You will quickly find yourself more appreciative of your own life and self.

Recap

It is quite simple to compare yourself to others anytime you are facing obstacles, but you must reject this tendency. Comparing oneself to others is detrimental to conquering obstacles, and it is impractical. Make a deliberate effort to quit comparing yourself to others to unlock greater success.

Chapter 7

LET'S TALK ABOUT EMOTIONAL RESILIENCE

Whenever you face any obstacle, it is simple to be carried away by your emotions and feel hopeless. When this occurs, it might be next to impossible to conquer the problem at hand. One approach to overcome these feelings is via emotional resilience.

What is Emotional Resilience?

Emotional resilience is the ability to relax oneself anytime you find yourself confronting an unpleasant situation. This terrible experience might be your feelings, an obstacle, or anything else that causes your thoughts and emotions to go crazy.

Everyone is born with a little amount of emotional resilience. That is how we are naturally able to deal with at least some stressful experiences. The older we become, our emotional resilience develops, helping us to face even more tough circumstances.

You may even purposefully build your emotional resilience via practices, self-compassion, and self-esteem. Improving your emotional resilience can help you overcome any obstacle that comes your way.

It may be beneficial to conceive of emotional resilience as a muscle. All healthy individuals are born with muscles. As we become larger, our muscles increase too. Some individuals even take the time to train and target certain muscles to get as strong as possible.

Whenever we find ourselves wanting to lift anything or impress a possible date, we may flex our muscles. In other words, we utilize our muscles all the time, yet we can flex them anytime we choose.

Our emotional resiliency is the same way. Emotional resilience helps us throughout the day, but it may be required more so during particular occurrences.

How Does Emotional Resilience Help You Overcome Obstacles?

Emotional resilience is crucial for not only surviving problems but translating them into success. It is only through emotional resilience that we believe we can endure obstacles and progress in our lives. This is a critical part of conquering challenges that you can't overlook.

Let's picture a life in which you had no emotional resilience. You can soon give up, weep, and become down on yourself because of the problem. You aren't able to regulate your thoughts or emotions, prohibiting you from conquering the difficulty. However, with emotional resilience, you would be able to calm your thoughts and logically communicate to yourself. This talent would then enable you to conceive of sensible solutions for overcoming the challenge and change it into success.

Elements of Emotional Resilience

The nice aspect of emotional resilience is that you can cultivate it. Whether you are very emotionally resilient or not, you can always learn a bit more. Overall, emotional resilience incorporates three aspects: physical elements, mental elements, and social elements. You must focus on all elements to improve your emotional resilience.

Physical elements include your energy, health, and vigor. If you are unwell and your body doesn't perform as it should, it is far more difficult to remain emotionally resilient. If you don't already, concentrate on eating healthy meals and getting some exercise to assist your emotional resilience.

The mental elements include your self-esteem, self-confidence, adaptability, emotional awareness, attention, self-expression, and reasoning skills. These factors are key to having excellent emotional resilience. You will need to perform a lot of personal effort to target this area, depending on your precise requirements.

For example, you can suffer from self-esteem yet be brilliant in your reasoning ability. If that's the case, you may want to go to a therapist to talk about the reasons you feel bad about yourself.

Others could have the opposite difficulty. They may have strong self-esteem but limited cognitive ability. Those folks may wish to start reading more to challenge their intellect.

Finally, the final aspect is social elements. This is your interpersonal interactions, communication skills, and cooperation. Humans are not created to be lone creatures. Boost your emotional resilience by expanding your relationships and communication abilities with others. They will come in helpful anytime you meet an obstacle.

Building Emotional Resilience

Whenever you wish to increase your emotional resilience, it is essential to address the three factors above. Some folks could need assistance with the relationship part yet be fantastic with the other two. Reflect on yourself to find out which areas you may need to enhance. Most individuals need to improve all three to some degree.

From there, you need to be watchful about your thoughts and behaviors. Notice anytime you feel horrible about yourself or whenever you feel like you lose control. As you are recognizing your thoughts and behaviors, practice talking yourself down and self-compassion.

Talking yourself down entails unwinding your ideas. See if there are any discrepancies or logical reasons that spring into your thoughts. Debunking these notions can help you arrive at a much more level-headed position.

In addition to concentrating on yourself, take the time to strengthen your relationships. This may be as easy as organizing a lunch with your parents, but it might also be as extensive as asking for support from a friend.

You may even want to chat about what you've been discovering in your search for self-reflection while improving your social ties. If you are finding increasing your emotional resilience to be particularly tough, try talking to a therapist or certified expert. These professionals will help you discover your issue thoughts and unwind them to increase your emotional resilience.

Recap

Emotional resilience is crucial to conquering any obstacle. Much like a muscle, your emotional resilience may be built by conscious thoughts and behaviors. Even if you are already emotionally resilient, continue to train this muscle to help convert any obstacle into a success

Chapter 8

TURN CHALLENGES INTO SUCCESS

Finally, we have reached the final chapter of this book. So far, we have spoken about the reality of obstacles and how perception and the false sense of control primarily impact your capacity to overcome them. We've also spoken about recognizing obstacles, setting goals, focusing on yourself, and emotional resilience to help you find a way through your difficulty.

But how can you change an obstacle into success? After all, merely conquering the difficulty isn't the same as success. In this chapter, we are going to provide you with essential methods not only to overcome your obstacle but transform it into a powerful symbol of success in your life.

Practice, Practice, Practice

As the adage goes, practice makes perfect. To overcome any challenge that comes your way, you have to have experience in overcoming them. This implies that transforming obstacles into success could be tricky at first, but it will grow simpler as you progress. This is a natural reality of life.

Practice all of the suggestions above every time you confront an obstacle, no matter how little the difficulty may appear. Think of this as obstacle resilience training. This training will help you get into the habit of conquering difficulties to find out exactly what you need to work on within yourself.

If you don't feel like you have any difficulties to practice on, you definitely aren't searching hard enough. Obstacles are so common in our existence that most of them go ignored. Take a close look at your ordinary life, and you will undoubtedly notice an obstacle or two hidden there.

Don't Give Up

Some obstacles will be tougher than others. Make sure not to give up. Even if you feel stuck and that the strategy isn't working, continue pushing. Only with constant effort can you change obstacles into success.

Of course, this isn't the same as letting go when it's not worth it. If your instinct is telling you that you shouldn't be worrying too much about a given problem, then listen to it.

But do not quit merely because the task is hard, or you are terrified. Giving up out of fear can only harm you. Plus, you will surely regret it in the future, and life is too short to regret any decisions.

Stay Optimistic

One of the simplest ways to guarantee that you don't give up is to be positive. As we just stated, there is always at least one good to whatever obstacle you face. Keep these things in your mind's eye to remain hopeful.

In addition to keeping positive about the obstacles you face, stay optimistic about yourself too. If you believe that you struggle with self-confidence or self-worth, go to your doctor. These are critical concerns that need to be addressed.

Stay positive about your life as a whole as well. Even if you aren't exactly where you want to be yet, understand that you are closer to accomplishing your goal than ever before. This can help you remain excited about tackling your obstacles because you are already close to your final goal.

You're Not In The Clear Yet

Once you conquer the obstacle at hand, it may be easy to breathe a sigh of relief and assume you are in the clear. Though you should rejoice and be excited about conquering your obstacle, you are not in the clear yet.

As we have discussed many times throughout this book, difficulties are everywhere. Just because you overcame one does not guarantee that it will be easy sailing from here on out. Very soon, another challenge will come your way.

Be prepared for future obstacles by continuing to push yourself, even when you don't feel like it. This may seem excessive, but this persistent quest for better is what will convert your obstacles into success. Focus on yourself and your growth, even after the obstacle is over.

Recap

The only way to totally change an obstacle into success is to implement what you have learned from this book into your daily life. While you meet an obstacle and conquer it, continue to practice and push yourself to apply these methods. Only then will you witness a meaningful transformation inwardly, which will help you to flourish elsewhere in your life.

Conclusion

Obstacles are an essential part of life, yet they may be tremendously tough. Learning to overcome an obstacle may put you under a lot of social or financial strain. On top of that, obstacles challenge your emotional and mental acuity, forcing some to crumble under pressure.

However, with work and attention, you can overcome obstacles and convert them into success.

Just by acknowledging that there are benefits to obstacles and that your perspective counts, you take away a lot of the power of obstacles. Furthermore, realizing that you are not in perfect control limits the number of obstacles you may confront.

From there, you may tackle any obstacle with a level mind and a modicum of rationality. This helps you to identify obstacles and set goals for an act to follow through. As you make attempts to reach your goals, concentrate on yourself and improve your emotional resilience. Just by doing this, you are nearly sure to conquer any obstacle.

The actual measure of success is how the challenge affects you and causes you to develop. The only way you can change the obstacle into success is by ingraining the lessons learned into your mind and enhancing your life. Continue to practice, keep cheerful, and develop yourself to transform every obstacle into a chance for success.

I'm going to warn you. The path is not going to be easy. There are going to be moments when you want to give up and believe that all your hard work is pointless. It is during such moments that you need to be motivated and thrilled the most. Keep your chin up, and you are going to be converting obstacles into success and unlock your full potential in no time.